Selfishness

RESOURCES FOR BIBLICAL LIVING

Lou Priolo, series editor

Selfishness

*From Loving Yourself to
Loving Your Neighbor*

LOU PRIOLO

PUBLISHING
P.O. BOX 817 • PHILLIPSBURG • NEW JERSEY 08865-0817

WHEN I USED TO read these words written by the apostle Paul, I assumed that they were describing the characteristics of pagan societies:

> But realize this, that in the last days difficult times will come. For men will be *lovers of self*, lovers of money, boastful, arrogant, revilers, disobedient to parents, ungrateful, unholy, unloving, irreconcilable, malicious gossips, without self-control, brutal, haters of good, treacherous, reckless, conceited, lovers of pleasure rather than lovers of God, holding to a form of godliness, although they have denied its power; avoid such men as these. (2 Tim. 3:1–5)

But then I realized, as the verses surrounding this passage indicate, that Paul was warning Timothy about the characteristics of those who would be *within the church* in the last days. Think of it—these are the kinds of problem people who attend church with you on a regular basis. There is even a chance that this passage might, in one way or another, describe you. But that's OK, because, in the pages that follow, you will learn how to deal with the one sin that spawns them all.

Notice the first description of these individuals: they are lovers of self. This phrase is the big umbrella under which all of the other characteristics of the last days dwell. It is from the *love of self* that all the other inordinate loves flow. As John Calvin said:

> We shall never love our neighbors with sincerity, according to our Lord's intention, until we have corrected the love of ourselves. The two affections are opposite and contradictory; for

the love of ourselves leads us to neglect and despise others,—produces cruelty, covetousness, violence, deceit, and all kindred vices,—drives us to impatience, and arms us with the desire of revenge.[1]

Perhaps it has been years since you took a college entrance exam, such as the SAT. I would like to ask you to take a revised version of the SAT. This version is not the Standard Aptitude Test, but rather the Selfish Attitude Test.

Selfish Attitude Test

RATING SCALE	POINTS
NEVER (HARDLY EVER)	5
SELDOM	4
SOMETIMES	3
FREQUENTLY	2
ALWAYS (ALMOST ALWAYS)	1

Give yourself a rating of 1 to 5 for each question:

1. When making decisions, I consider only how the decision will benefit me, rather than how the decision might benefit others and how the decision can most glorify God.
2. I believe that friendships are more trouble than they're worth.
3. I spend more time thinking about my favorite temporal delight than I do thinking about God, his Word, or delights of eternal significance.
4. I am more concerned about promoting my interests than God's interests.
5. I think about how others don't love or appreciate me.
6. When people hurt or offend me, I write them off and have little or nothing to do with them.

1. John Calvin, *Commentaries on the Epistles of Paul to the Galatians and Ephesians* (repr., Grand Rapids: Baker Book House, 1993), 161.

7. I think about how nice it would be to have others serve me.
8. I become anxious and fearful when I am not in control of my own surroundings.
9. I am more competitive than I should be.
10. When meeting a new person, I spend more time thinking about how to impress him or her than how to minister to him or her.
11. I do not witness to others as I should, due to my fear of being criticized or rejected.
12. I long to be noticed more than I long to be godly.
13. I overreact to criticism by dwelling too long on it or allowing it to depress me unnecessarily.
14. I have a fear of being rejected that keeps me from getting close to others.
15. I find it difficult to rejoice when I see others blessed with the things that I dearly want.
16. I find it difficult to rejoice when others are given the honor and recognition which I believe I deserve.
17. I am a taker rather than a giver.
18. I have great difficulty submitting my will to God's will.
19. I am stingier than I ought to be.
20. I am overprotective of those I love.

Add up your total number of points. That will give you a general idea of how selfish you really are. Scores range from 20 (completely selfish) to 100 (completely unselfish).[2]

What Is Selfishness?

How would you define selfishness? What does it look like? How would you explain it to others? To what Bible

---

2. This SAT inventory is, obviously, not a scientifically normed instrument. Because the questions were developed from biblical constructs, persons taking the test are being compared more closely to the character of Jesus Christ than to the character of those in our secular society.

passages would you turn to learn about this problem that plagues us all? Let me suggest a few answers to these important questions.

Selfishness is the lack (or opposite) of biblical love.

The essence of love is giving:

> Husbands, love your wives, just as Christ also loved the church and *gave* Himself up for her. (Eph. 5:25)

> For God so loved the world, that He *gave* His only begotten Son, that whoever believes in Him shall not perish, but have eternal life. (John 3:16)

> Walk in love, just as Christ also loved you, and *gave* Himself up for us, an offering and a sacrifice to God as a fragrant aroma. (Eph. 5:2)

> I have been crucified with Christ; it is no longer I who live, but Christ lives in me; and the life which I now live in the flesh I live by faith in the Son of God, who loved me and *gave* Himself for me. (Gal. 2:20 NKJV)

Jesus tells us to love our enemies:

> You have heard that it was said, "You shall love your neighbor and hate your enemy." But I say to you, *love your enemies* and pray for those who persecute you. (Matt. 5:43–44)

Solomon tells us how to do it:

> If your enemy is hungry, *give* him food to eat;
> And if he is thirsty, *give* him water to drink. (Prov. 25:21)

Now consider the verse that immediately precedes what is arguably the best description of love in the Bible:

8

And if I *give* all my possessions to feed the poor, and if I surrender [i.e., *give*] my body to be burned, *but do not have love*, it profits me nothing. (1 Cor. 13:3)

It is possible to give away all of your personal possessions and still not have love. And it is possible to make the ultimate sacrifice and give up (lay down) your own life and yet not have love.

Love involves giving without having a selfish primary *motive* for doing so.[3] Selfishness is being more concerned with (interested in or motivated by) what I can get from others than with what I can give to them.

> Do not eat the bread of a selfish man,
> Or desire his delicacies;
> For as he thinks within himself, so he is.
> He says to you, "Eat and drink!"
> But his heart is not with you.
> You will vomit up the morsel you have eaten,
> And waste your compliments. (Prov. 23:6–8)

The same principle may, in part, be applied to our love for God. As Richard Baxter, the prolific Puritan writer put it,

> Wherever the interest of carnal self is stronger than and more predominant habitually than the interest of God, of Christ, of everlasting life, there is no true self-denial . . . but where God's interest is the strongest, there self-denial is sincere.[4]

He says of selfishness in another place that it "is the radical, positive sin of the soul, comprehending seminally [i.e., in seed form]

---

3. Love focuses its attention on the *needs* of others, not necessarily their *wants*. In Luke 10, for example, Martha apparently thought she needed something that she really didn't—help in the kitchen. Like her sister Mary, what she really needed was to sit at the feet of Jesus and hear his words.

4. Richard Baxter, *The Practical Works of Richard Baxter*, 4 vols. (repr., Ligonier, PA: Soli Deo Gloria Publications, 1990–2000), 3:392.

and causally all the rest."[5] That is to say, our greatest *sin of commission*, out of which all others flow, is selfishness. Practically speaking, it is the selfishness in our hearts that generates all our other sins. This brings us to our second definition of selfishness.

Selfishness is, for all intents and purposes, the practical equivalent of sin.

James writes:

> Let no one say when he is tempted, "I am being tempted by God"; for God cannot be tempted by evil, and He Himself does not tempt any one. But each one is tempted when he is carried away and enticed by his own lust. Then when lust has conceived, it gives birth to sin; and when sin is accomplished, it brings forth death. (James 1:13–15)

Idolatrous desires in your heart are like a two-sided coin. On one side, the coin reads *selfishness*. On the other side, the coin reads *lack of love for God and neighbor*. That is our greatest *sin of omission*. Here's the way Baxter put it: "Man's fall was his turning from God to himself; and his regeneration consisteth in the turning of him from himself to God . . . and the mortifying of self love. Selfishness therefore is all positive sin in one, as want of the love of God is all privitive sin in one."[6]

Because man is sinful (i.e., selfish), God's practical remedy is for him to learn how to love God and to love his neighbor:

> One of them, a lawyer, asked Him a question, testing Him, "Teacher, which is the great commandment in the Law?" And He said to him, "'You shall love the Lord your God with all your heart, and with all your soul, and with all your mind.' This is the great and foremost commandment. The second is like it, 'You shall love your neighbor as yourself.' On these two commandments depend the whole Law and the Prophets." (Matt. 22:35–40)

5. Baxter, *Practical Works*, 1:868.
6. Baxter, *Practical Works*, 1:868–69.

These two great commandments, on which all the others depend,[7] are the two greatest practical antidotes for indwelling sin. The more you love God and your neighbor, the less selfish (sinful) you will be. Because man is sinful (selfish), God's remedy is for him to learn how to love God and love his neighbor. The New Testament emphasizes love because love is the single best antidote for sin.

"Selfishness," as a one-word definition of sin, is, of course, theologically inaccurate, largely because it doesn't include the idea that the transgression is committed against a holy God. But, from a practical perspective (that of progressive sanctification), this is probably as close as you can come in one word.

Selfishness is "the mother of all sins." As we have seen (2 Tim. 3:1–5), it is the one sin out of which most of the others seem to flow. It is the one sin that is most common to man. Baxter believed that selfishness (love of self) is the quintessence (or epitome) of idolatry:

> I have formerly told you, that self is the god of wicked men, or the world's greatest idol; and that the inordinate love of pleasure, profits and honor, in trinity, is all but this self love in unity. . . . Every man is an idolater, so far as he is selfish. . . . Now selfish ungodly men do all of them rob God, and give His honor and prerogatives to themselves. . . . They call him their God, but will not have Him for . . . their portion . . . nor give Him the strongest love of their hearts: they will not take Him as their absolute owner; and devote themselves and all they have to Him. . . . They will not take Him for their Sovereign, and be ruled by Him, nor deny themselves for Him, nor seek His honor and interest above their own. They call Him their father, but deny Him his honor; and [they call Him] their master, but give Him not His fear. They depend not on His hand, and live not *by* His law, and *to* His glory; and therefore do not take Him for their God.[8]

---

7. In one way or another, selfishness is at the heart of the breaking of each of the Ten Commandments.

8. Baxter, *Practical Works*, 3:379.

Selfishness is directly related to sinful fear.[9]

Have you ever examined the correlation between selfishness and sinful fear? People who are selfish tend to be fearful. People who are fearful are necessarily selfish. I know that last statement is a rather strong one, but let's try to think biblically about this matter. What is the biblical antithesis of fear? According to Scripture, the opposite of (and remedy to) sinful fear is love: "There is no fear in love; but perfect love casts out fear, because fear involves punishment, and the one who fears is not perfected in love" (1 John 4:18).

But love is also antithetical to (as well as the antidote for) the sin of selfishness. We know this, not only because 1 Corinthians 13:5, says that love "does not seek its own," but also because the essence of love is giving and the essence of selfishness is taking. So if we could express this in the form of an equation, it would look something like this:

$$\frac{\text{Fear} \quad \text{is the opposite of} \quad \text{Love}}{\text{Love} \quad \text{is the opposite of} \quad \text{Selfishness}}$$

The relationship between fear and selfishness becomes apparent by simply factoring out the "love" from both sides of the equation:

$$\frac{\text{Fear} \quad \text{is the opposite of} \quad \text{Love}}{\text{Love} \quad \text{is the opposite of} \quad \text{Selfishness}} = \frac{\text{Love}}{\text{Selfishness}} = \frac{\text{Fear}}{\text{Selfishness}}$$

If you truly love someone, you'll be more concerned with what you can give to him than with what you can get from him. Consider Baxter's thoughts on the inverse relationship between one's self-interest and interest in things of God: "Wherever the interest of carnal self is stronger than and more predominant

9. Material in this section has been adapted from the author's previous booklet, *Fear: Breaking Its Grip* (Phillipsburg, NJ: P&R Publishing, 2009).

habitually than the interest of God, of Christ, of everlasting life, there is no true self-denial or saving grace; but where God's interest is the strongest, there self-denial is sincere."[10]

William Kilpatrick, in his book *Psychological Seduction*, makes the point that extreme forms of mental illness are always extreme cases of self-absorption:

> The distinctive quality, the thing that literally sets *paranoid* [biblical term: *fearful*] people apart, is hyper self-consciousness. And the thing they prize most about themselves is *autonomy*. Their constant fear is that someone else is interfering with their will or trying to direct their lives. For this type of person, self-abandonment is the worst fate. Rather than have that happen, they draw deeper into themselves, cutting the cords of sociability as they go.[11]

We might even say that the problem with most crazy persons is that they're crazy about themselves.

Selfishness is superimposing my will on God's will—that is, being self-willed.

Much has been said in the evangelical community about the strong-willed individual. But when was the last time you heard someone speak about the self-willed individual? Paul says:

> For the overseer must be above reproach as God's steward, *not self-willed*, not quick-tempered, not addicted to wine, not pugnacious, not fond of sordid gain. (Titus 1:7)

The unselfish individual is *willing* to subordinate his own interests and desires to God's:

> Then I said, "Behold, I come;
> In the scroll of the book it is written of me.

10. Baxter, *Practical Works*, 3:392.
11. William Kilpatrick, *Psychological Seduction* (Nashville: T. Nelson, 1983), 67.

I delight to do *Your will*, O my God;
Your Law is within my heart." (Ps. 40:7–8)

Father, if You are willing, remove this cup from Me; yet *not My will, but Yours be done*. (Luke 22:42)

Of all the organs of the soul, the will is afflicted by the disease of selfishness more than any other.[12] Baxter writes:

> The will of man is the terrestrial throne of God. It is there that He must reign. The will is to rule all the inferior faculties; and God is to rule the will. And shall self presume to dethrone the Lord, and sit down in His place? He that rules the will rules the man.[13]

Has following your own will not yet proven to you how much misery and pain result when you do so? How many times have you wished that you had obeyed the Lord's will rather than following your own?

I will sometimes ask self-willed individuals this question: "Do you want to know God's will to *do* it or to *vote on* it?"

Whenever I do something selfish, inevitably it is because I am being self-willed—I was more concerned with what I wanted to do than what the Lord wanted me to do. How about you?

Suggestions for Overcoming Selfishness (and Dethroning the Idol of Self-love)

It should go without saying that none of us is capable of stopping the surge of any sin, let alone this source of all sin,

---

12. By "organs of the soul," I mean those internal organs of biblical anthropology such as passions or desires, emotions, conscience, thoughts, and imaginations. Selfishness corrupts all of these faculties.

13. Baxter, *Practical Works*, 3:400.

apart from the sanctifying work of the Spirit.[14] Indeed, the first fruit of the Spirit is love (the very antidote to this poison that flows in all of our veins). So please resist the temptation to see the scriptural applications that follow as something you can do in your own power to bring about your own renewal or happiness. Apart from Christ, you and I can do nothing—except make matters worse.

As with much of the contents of this booklet, I have relied heavily on the works of Richard Baxter. All of the citations in this section, unless otherwise noted, are his (I have taken the liberty to paraphrase some of them).

Understand the horrific nature and broad scope of the sin of selfishness.

Never lose sight of the fact that selfishness is the one sin out of which all others flow. To mortify selfishness is to subdue the chief enemy of your soul. It is to remove from the Devil the greatest handle by which he attempts to influence and seduce us. James writes:

> But if you have bitter jealousy and selfish ambition in your heart, do not be arrogant and so lie against the truth. This wisdom is not that which comes down from above, but is earthly, natural, demonic. For where jealousy and *selfish* ambition exist, there is *disorder* and *every evil thing*. (James 3:14–16)

Consider the perfections of the glorious God you serve and the purposes for which he saved you, and then remind yourself often

14. A. A. Hodge explains: "It must be remembered that while the subject is passive with respect to that divine act of grace whereby he is regenerated, after he is regenerated he co-operates with the Holy Ghost in the work of sanctification. The Holy Ghost gives the grace, and prompts and directs in its exercise, and the soul exercises it. Thus, while sanctification is a grace, it is also a duty; and the soul is both bound and encouraged to use with diligence, in dependence upon the Holy Spirit, all the means for its spiritual renovation, and to form those habits of resisting evil and of right action in which sanctification so largely consists" (*The Confession of Faith* [1869; repr., London: Banner of Truth Trust, 1958], 196).

how exceedingly more qualified he is than you are to govern your life.

Think about God's attributes: his omnipotence, omniscience, omnipresence, justice, faithfulness, wisdom, goodness, and love—to name a few. And don't forget his sovereignty:

> The LORD has established His throne in the heavens,
> And His *sovereignty rules* over all. (Ps. 103:19)

> He who is the blessed and only *Sovereign*, the King of kings and Lord of lords, who alone possesses immortality and dwells in unapproachable light, whom no man has seen or can see. To Him be honor and eternal dominion! Amen. (1 Tim. 6:15–16)

Do you really think you are more capable to run the affairs of your own life than God is? He has saved you and predestined you to be conformed to the image of Christ. Do you really think you can improve on that?

> Thine own will is a corrupt and sinful will, and therefore unfit to be thy governor: *What! Wilt thou choose an unjust, a wicked, an unmerciful governor that is inclined to do evil?* . . . To prefer self will before the will of God, is as the Jews, to prefer a murderer, Barabbas, before the Lord of life. . . . When God is content to be your governor, prefer not such foolish sinners as yourself before Him.[15]

Set your heart on diligently seeking the love of Christ (because in so doing selfishness will flee).

We are so selfish—that is, our love of self is so strong—that a love much stronger than our own is required to overpower it. To the degree (and only to that degree) that we truly comprehend Christ's love for us and make it our goal to show his love

15. Baxter, *Practical Works*, 3:400–401.

to others, we will conquer our selfishness. It is the love of Christ that controls us (2 Cor. 5:14). It is a four-dimensional love that exceeds our natural ability to understand:

> That you, being rooted and grounded in love, may be able to comprehend with all the saints what is the *breadth* and *length* and *height* and *depth*, and to know the love of Christ which *surpasses knowledge*, that you may be filled up to all the fullness of God. (Eph. 3:17–19)

This requires the Holy Spirit first to open our eyes and pour Christ's love out within our hearts (Rom. 5:5). Again, self-love can be effectively conquered only by a more powerful love. Baxter observes:

> Men will not be frightened by self-love. It must be another more powerful love that will draw them from it—and that can be none other than the love of God. When you have soundly discerned a surer friend than self, a wiser, a wise, a better, an abler governor and defender, and one who is much more deserving of all your love and attention, then you will turn away from self, but never until then.[16]

I sometimes utilize a glass that sits next to a pitcher of cold water on my desk when explaining the important "put off, put on" dynamic to those I counsel. "This glass represents your heart," I say. Then, after filling the glass halfway with water, I continue, "If I wanted to empty this glass and prevent someone from refilling it, I'd have to do more than simply empty it. I would have to fill it with something heavier than water, such as sand—or better yet, some kind of dense, waterproof epoxy that would harden a few minutes after it was poured. If I add the epoxy to the water, it will sink to the bottom of the glass. Little by little, the glass will begin to fill from the bottom. The

16. Baxter, *Practical Works*, 3:473 (paraphrased).

water will be displaced and begin to spill out over the top of the glass until it has been completely replaced by the epoxy. Once the epoxy hardens, it will be very difficult for anyone to put water in the glass again.

"So it is with the sin in our lives. We displace the sin in our heart by replacing it with something better—something biblically heavier, stronger, and more durable than the sin."[17]

The point I want to drive home to my counselees is that with some sins, the "put on" is the most effective means of accomplishing the "put off." The goal of my instruction is to help people put on love (cf. 1 Tim. 1:5). The commandment to love is exalted above all others (Mark 12:30–31). Love is the most important motivation for all of us—not just our love for God, but, more importantly, his love for us. It is the love of Christ that constrains us. We love him because he first loved us.

Saturate your mind with those portions of Scripture that describe and explain both self-love and its biblical antidote, agape love.

The single most important way that you and I can cooperate with the Holy Spirit's sanctifying work in our lives is by getting his Word into our hearts (cf. Col. 3:16):

How can a young man keep his way pure?
By keeping it according to Your word.
With all my heart I have sought You;
Do not let me wander from Your commandments.
Your word I have treasured in my heart,
That I may not sin against You. (Ps. 119:9–11)

In addition to the classic 1 Corinthians 13 passage, here are some other passages you may want to consider internalizing.

17. The content of this illustration has been adapted from the author's previous booklet, *Fear: Breaking Its Grip* (Phillipsburg, NJ: P&R Publishing, 2009).

Suggested portions of Scripture for memorization to overcome selfishness	
Luke 6:31–35	Treat others the same way you want them to treat you. If you love those who love you, what credit is that to you? For even sinners love those who love them. If you do good to those who do good to you, what credit is that to you? For even sinners do the same. If you lend to those from whom you expect to receive, what credit is that to you? Even sinners lend to sinners in order to receive back the same amount. But love your enemies, and do good, and lend, expecting nothing in return; and your reward will be great, and you will be sons of the Most High; for He Himself is kind to ungrateful and evil men.
John 15:7–15	If you abide in Me, and My words abide in you, ask whatever you wish, and it will be done for you. My Father is glorified by this, that you bear much fruit, and so prove to be My disciples. Just as the Father has loved Me, I have also loved you; abide in My love. If you keep My commandments, you will abide in My love; just as I have kept My Father's commandments and abide in His love. These things I have spoken to you so that My joy may be in you, and that your joy may be made full. This is My commandment, that you love one another, just as I have loved you. Greater love has no one than this, that one lay down his life for his friends. You are My friends if you do what I command you. No longer do I call you slaves, for the slave does not know what his master is doing; but I have called you friends, for all things that I have heard from My Father I have made known to you.
Rom. 12:9–10	Let love be without hypocrisy. Abhor what is evil; cling to what is good. Be devoted to one another in brotherly love; give preference to one another in honor.
Rom. 15:1–3	Now we who are strong ought to bear the weaknesses of those without strength and not just please ourselves. Each of us is to please his neighbor for his good, to his edification. For even Christ did not please Himself; but as it is written, "The reproaches of those who reproached You fell on Me."

2 Cor. 8:9	For you know the grace of our Lord Jesus Christ, that though He was rich, yet for your sake He became poor, so that you through His poverty might become rich.
1 Cor. 10:24, 31-33	Let no one seek his own good, but that of his neighbor. . . . Whether, then, you eat or drink or whatever you do, do all to the glory of God. Give no offense either to Jews or to Greeks or to the church of God; just as I also please all men in all things, not seeking my own profit but the profit of the many, so that they may be saved.
2 Cor. 5:14-15	For the love of Christ controls us, having concluded this, that one died for all, therefore all died; and He died for all, so that they who live might no longer live for themselves, but for Him who died and rose again on their behalf.
Phil. 2:1-11	Therefore if there is any encouragement in Christ, if there is any consolation of love, if there is any fellowship of the Spirit, if any affection and compassion, make my joy complete by being of the same mind, maintaining the same love, united in spirit, intent on one purpose. Do nothing from selfishness or empty conceit, but with humility of mind regard one another as more important than yourselves; do not merely look out for your own personal interests, but also for the interests of others. Have this attitude in yourselves which was also in Christ Jesus, who, although He existed in the form of God, did not regard equality with God a thing to be grasped, but emptied Himself, taking the form of a bondservant, and being made in the likeness of men. Being found in appearance as a man, He humbled Himself by becoming obedient to the point of death, even death on a cross. For this reason also, God highly exalted Him, and bestowed on Him the name which is above every name, so that at the name of Jesus every knee will bow, of those who are in heaven and on earth and under the earth, and that every tongue will confess that Jesus Christ is Lord, to the glory of God the Father.
James 2:15-16	If a brother or sister is without clothing and in need of daily food, and one of you says to them, "Go in peace, be warmed and be filled," and yet you do not give them what is necessary for their body, what use is that?

Consider (meditate on) how you ought to demonstrate your love for God and neighbor.

Meditation is a lost art. Actually, it is much more than that. It is God's means to prosperity and success:

> This book of the law shall not depart from your mouth, but you shall meditate on it day and night, so that you may be careful to do according to all that is written in it; for then you will make your way prosperous, and then you will have success. (Josh. 1:8)

Here is what Oliver Heywood said about it over three hundred years ago:

> Christian meditation is the contemplative and earnest fixing of the mind on the great spiritual realities which the Bible has revealed to us. . . . Meditation is the soul's conference with itself; the discourse which it holds with truth obtained, and impressions received, in the secret sanctuary of its own consciousness. It is the . . . solemn endeavor of the soul to bring home to itself divine things; and so to resolve, ponder, and digest them, as to work their transforming power into every element and faculty of its being. . . . It is the digestive process, by which spiritual food nourishes the soul and promotes its growth in holiness.
>
> Lack of meditation is the primary reason that so many professing Christians, in spite of exposure to the most excellent teaching, still remain ignorant, unstable, and unfruitful; "ever learning, but never able to come to the knowledge of the truth." Instruction flows in upon them from all sides; but their hearts and minds are like sieves, out of which everything runs as fast as it is poured in. The impressions which truth makes on their minds, are as temporary as characters traced on the sands of the sea-shore, which the next wave erases forever. But meditation *imprints truth deeply* on the conscience, and *engraves* it on the tablets of "the inner man," "as with the point of a diamond or a laser beam." It thus becomes incorporated into the soul;

and forms, as it were, a part of it; and it is ever present, to regulate the heart's affections and to control and guide all of its movements."[18]

May I suggest a little project for you to consider? (It's actually a homework assignment that I sometimes give to those who are struggling with selfishness.) It is based on 1 Corinthians 13:4–7, where we find a description of what love *does*. As we have seen from the biblical perspective, love is more of a verb than a noun. There are fifteen descriptive verbs about love found in verses 4–7 of this famous "love chapter."[19] Eight of the fifteen are stated negatively (love is/does not . . .); seven are stated positively (love is/does . . .). The negative descriptions imply their positive counterparts, and the positive descriptions imply their negative counterparts (lack of love). In other words, being patient with someone means that you will not be impatient, and "not seeking its own" implies that love will seek the interests of the person who is being loved.

Begin by identifying one or two of the closest people ("neighbors") in your life (those you are most obligated to love) with whom you have been most selfish. Then, for every person, write the descriptions of love across the top of fifteen sheets of paper (one description per page).[20] Then try to come up with at least four or five specific manifestations of (practical applications for) each of the fifteen elements. Here are a couple of examples.

Love Is Patient

I can demonstrate *patience* to my wife by:

18. Adapted and paraphrased from Oliver Heywood, *Heart Treasure* (1667), vol. 2 of *The Whole Works of the Rev. Oliver Heywood* (1825; repr., Morgan, PA: Soli Deo Gloria, 1997), 250ff.

19. The list is sufficient, but not exhaustive. There are other aspects of love found elsewhere in the Bible that are not mentioned here. For example, love is not fearful (1 John 4:18).

20. Or, as an alternative, you can do this on a word processor, placing the descriptions at the top of fifteen pages of the document.

- ☐ not getting angry when she isn't ready to leave on time.
- ☐ calmly answering her when she questions my reasons for doing something.
- ☐ not retaliating when she gives me the cold shoulder.
- ☐ not expecting her to change her bad habits overnight.
- ☐ being understanding when she doesn't fulfill my requests within the desired time frame.

Love Is Kind

I can demonstrate *kindness* to my wife by:

- ☐ agreeing with her when she is pointing out my weaknesses.
- ☐ talking respectfully to her while she is speaking disrespectfully to me.
- ☐ express sympathy when she doesn't feel well.
- ☐ helping her with her domestic responsibilities without having been asked.

Finally, practice two or three of these loving actions *every day* for each person you have targeted.

Learn how to make decisions, considering not only how the decision will benefit you, but also how the decision might benefit others and how it can most glorify God.

> Do nothing from selfishness or empty conceit, but with humility of mind regard one another as more important than yourselves; do not merely look out for your own personal interests, but also for the interests of others. (Phil. 2:3–4)

Ask yourself, "Is there not a more excellent way, a more excellent end or purpose that would glorify God or benefit my neighbor?" before you finalize your decisions. See if you can come up with five or six similar self-evaluation questions.

Commit yourself to following the dynamic of 1 John 4:18—not to let fear paralyze and prevent you from obeying God, but rather to learn how to cast out fear by replacing it with love.

There is no fear in love; but perfect love casts out fear, because fear involves punishment, and the one who fears is not perfected in love. (1 John 4:18)

Many summers ago, I had the opportunity to work as a hired hand on a farm in Nebraska. I had to do whatever my boss needed for me to do on any given day: disk a field with a tractor, round up runaway cattle on a horse, adjust the irrigation pipes (from a three-wheeler)—you name it, I probably did it that summer.

One day my boss (who was a Christian) informed me that we were going to put up a television antenna. In those days, putting up an antenna on a rooftop in rural Nebraska was not sufficient to pull in many stations. So we had to erect (assemble) a fifty-foot triangular tower upon which to place the antenna.

Now you must understand that I am, to put it mildly, slightly acrophobic (fearful of high places). So the thought of clinging to a pole fifty feet off the ground struck terror in my heart. When I explained to my boss that I was afraid of heights, he pulled out a safety belt and told me not to worry. I then made another appeal, explaining that the belt didn't alleviate my fear of falling. To that he responded, "You are my hired hand, and this is what I need to do today." His implication was clear to me: "Lou, it's obviously God's will for you to go up there with me." At that point, I went into 1 John 4:18 mode. "If I love God and I love my boss, I will have to do what they want me to do. I am not going to let my fear of heights keep me from loving them. OK, Lord, please help me (and protect me) as I do your will."

Section by section we erected the tower. Yard by yard I prayed, and focused my attention on pleasing my boss. Before

24

I knew it, we were on the last section (the one with the antenna connected to it). But we couldn't get one of the three legs to align with (and fit into) the previous section.

"I'm going to have to go up higher; let me have your belt," my boss said to me.

"Are you kidding? I'm almost five stories off the ground and you want me to give up my safety belt?" I screamed to myself.

"Here, take this," he said, as he handed me the belt from his trousers. "You can work your way down to the ground; I will try to get the last section seated by myself." (He probably wanted me out of the way, so I wouldn't get clobbered when the antenna fell to the ground. It didn't.) I made it down to the ground safely, thanking God for keeping me safe and enabling me to overcome my fear. A few minutes later, my boss successfully secured the last piece of the antenna and climbed down the tower. This experience convinced me of the power of the dynamic of 1 John 4:18—the power of love.

Study the examples in Scripture of Christ's sacrificial love for his church.

> For you know the grace of our Lord Jesus Christ, that though He was rich, yet for your sake He became poor, so that you through His poverty might become rich. (2 Cor. 8:9)

> Let Christ be your continual focus. He is the full revelation of the love of God; the lively pattern of love, and the best teacher of it that there has ever been in the world: His incarnation, life and sufferings, His Gospel and covenant, His intercession and preparations for our heavenly happiness. All are the great demonstrations of humble, matchless love. Keep your eyes on both God's love to us in Him, and His love to man, and you will have the best instruction and incentive for your love.[21]

21. Baxter, *Practical Works*, 1:872 (paraphrased).

Another project you might consider is to go through the Bible and study the specific ways in which Christ demonstrated his love for the church. (In light of Ephesians 5:25–33, this is an especially good assignment for husbands.) Here is a worksheet you can use if you like.

SPECIFIC WAYS CHRIST LOVES THE CHURCH

As you read through the New Testament, see how many examples of Christ's love for the church you can find. Record these in the first column. In the second column, record the interpretation or explanation of exactly how Christ demonstrated his love for his bride. In the third column, record how many personal applications of the passage you can make to the person you are attempting to love. Remember that although there may be many ways to apply a passage of Scripture (column 3), there is only one interpretation (column two) of Scripture: the one intended by the Holy Spirit (cf. 2 Peter 1:20).

Scripture Reference	How Christ Loves the Church	Application: How I can show love to _____.
1. Rom. 5:6–8	1. While they were yet sinners	1. By quickly forgiving him/her the next time he/she sins.
2. 1 John 4:19	2. He initiated love.	2. By taking the initiative to _____ and to _____.
3. John 3:16	3.	3.
4. Eph. 5:2	4.	4.
5. Matt. 20:28	5.	5.
6. John 15:13	6.	6.
7.	7.	7.
8.	8.	8.
9.	9.	9.
10.	10.	10.

Make it your goal to be a giver rather than a taker.

Remember the words of the Lord Jesus, that He Himself said, "It is more blessed to give than to receive." (Acts 20:35)

What can you give that you've been selfishly keeping to yourself? Your time? Your money? Your talents? Your food? Your home? Your toys (amusements)? Your affection? Your communication?

Why not spend five minutes every day prayerfully considering what and how you can give to those whom God has placed in your path (cf. Luke 10:30–37). For example, a husband on his way to the office might purposefully think of how he could encourage one or more of his coworkers. On the way home from work, he might think of how he could give of his time to his wife or children.

Follow the counsel of Christ to the Ephesians in Revelation 2:1–5.

Therefore remember from where you have fallen, and repent and do the deeds you did at first. (Rev. 2:5)

The church at Ephesus, you will remember, had lost their first love. The counsel given to them by Christ is most instructive for any counselee who needs to recover lost love (or develop love he never had). Notice that the counsel was not based on an emotional view of love. The Lord did not instruct them to "reach down into the depths of your 'love cup' and stir up a big fat warm fuzzy." Rather, he told them to do three things:

Remember (the way things were and the things they did when they were in love with him).[22]

Repent (change their minds and the direction of their life).

22. If you have never loved previously, you can "remember" by looking into the Scriptures (specifically 1 Cor. 13:4–7) to see what real loves does.

Do the deeds they did at first (do what the Bible says love does).

Prayerfully consider how to apply Christ's counsel to those whom you have failed to love.

Identify those persons to whom your selfishness has been most obnoxious and begin demonstrating genuine love to them.

> Zaccheus stopped and said to the Lord, "Behold, Lord, half of my possessions I will give to the poor, and if I have defrauded anyone of anything, I will give back four times as much." (Luke 19:8)

Do you remember the 1 Corinthians 13 exercise I described above? The project that follows is an expanded application of that exercise. Make a list of *all* the people you can think of who have been affected by your selfishness. Who has been hurt by your selfish actions and attitudes?

☐ Spouse
☐ Parents or children
☐ In-laws
☐ Employer or employees
☐ People at church
☐ Friends
☐ Former friends (enemies)
☐ Others (Can you think of anyone else with whom you've been especially selfish?)

When you have completed the list, add to it as many of the specific needs of each individual as you can think of. Then make a list of your personal resources (i.e., your spare time, prayer time, money, home and possessions, food, etc.). Finally, consider how to use the resources God has given you to meet the needs of those on your target list.

My Resources	People to Love	Their Needs	How to Use My Resources to Meet Their Needs

Let me conclude this booklet with a final quotation from Richard Baxter, who believed that selfishness is a universally stubborn sin:

> Selfishness is the hardest sin in the world to overcome. In all the unregenerate it is predominate; for nothing but the sanctifying Spirit of God can overcome it. And in many thousands that seem very zealous, in religion and very mortified [or self-disciplined], in all other respects, yet in some way or other selfishness doth so lamentably appear . . . and [it] is so strong in many that are sincere, that it is the greatest dishonor to the church of Christ . . . and [it] hath tempted many to infidelity, or to doubt whether there be any such thing as true sanctification in the world.[23]

Baxter is saying first that selfishness is predominant in the unsaved, and that it is impossible to overcome apart from the sanctifying work of the Holy Spirit. That is, the unregenerate don't have what it takes to overcome their own selfishness.[24] Second, selfishness is present in many zealous and otherwise holy Christians. And third, selfishness is apparent in so many believers who are sincerely following Christ that it disgraces him and tempts many to remain unconverted.

So, as you are cooperating with the Spirit of God to put to death this mother of all sins, don't forget that there is more at stake than just your own personal spiritual growth and reputation. People are watching and evaluating not just you, but your Lord.

Finally, there is a bit of irony in saying that selfishness is the mother of all sins, while trying to address this enormous problem in a small booklet. Much more can be (and in fact has been) written on this matter. So consider what you have

---

23. Baxter, *Practical Works*, 3:379.

24. Indeed, how can selfishness be put off and love be put on in its place by a person who has not yet had the love of God poured out in his heart (Rom. 5:5; cf. 1 John 4:19)?

just read as a sort of first chapter—something to cut your teeth on. Once you have mastered the few concepts that I have covered here, perhaps you will be better prepared to ponder the writings of Richard Baxter or Thomas Manton.[25] But until then, maybe the little bit of truth contained in this volume will at least get you oriented in the right direction. I pray that it will.

25. As of the publication date of this booklet, Baxter's *A Treatise of Self-Denial* is available at: http://books.google.com/books?ct=result&ie=ISO-88591&output=html&id=IYgfAAAAYAAJ&dq=%22richard+baxter%22+self+denial&ots=cSlPjbR1hG&jtp=355 and Manton's *A Treatise of Self-Denial* (yes, both books have the same title) is available at http://www.newblehome.co.uk/manton/vol15/self-denial.html.